The Earth

Some parts of the earth's surface have been drowned beneath the seas. Other parts have been raised up and are gradually being worn away by water, wind and ice. Man has lived on these raised areas for not much more than a million years.

The rocks forming the land on which early man lived had been created and shaped by nature. The kind of vegetation which grew depended on the soils which formed on these rocks and on the climate of the area.

Then man began to learn to use the rocks themselves. At first Stone Age Man simply used stones as weapons. Then he learned how to make them into knives and arrow-heads. Soon he began to shape the landscape itself. He made tools from the rocks to clear the trees and plough the land. He used stones for building, and he mined tin, copper, and iron. Later, he discovered the use of coal, petroleum, and radioactive minerals for power. Many of man's great achievements are directly linked to the rocks of the earth.

What the earth is made of

The *crust*, or outer layer, of the earth is made of separate blocks of solid rock. In relation to the rest of the earth, it is about as thick as the skin on a tomato. At the highest parts of the continents the crust is about 65 kilometres thick. Under the oceans it is very thin. Scientists think that a new crust may be forming here.

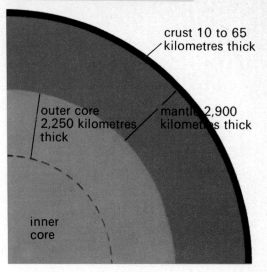

The structure of the earth

1. Make a large drawing of the area inside the rectangle on the diagram below. Add the following information to your drawing: 'The crust is very thin beneath the sea.' 'The crust is thicker beneath the continents.' 'The continental shelf is the edge of the continent under the sea.'

The outer part of the crust, forming the continents, is called the *sial*. It is made mostly of the minerals silicon and aluminium. When the molten earth cooled the sial rose to the top because it was lighter. It rests like a great raft on another layer called the *sima*. The sima is made of silicon and magnesium.

Beneath the crust the rocks change. The point where this occurs is called a *discontinuity*. It is named the Moho, after Andrija Mohorovičić, the Yugoslavian scientist who discovered it. Scientists once planned to drill through the crust to the rocks beneath. They called the plan the Mohole project. The core of the earth, even deeper down, is thought to be made of nickel and iron.

ocean deep

Mohorovičić Discontinuity

continental block (Sial)

mantle

basalt (Sima)

A closer look at the earth's crust

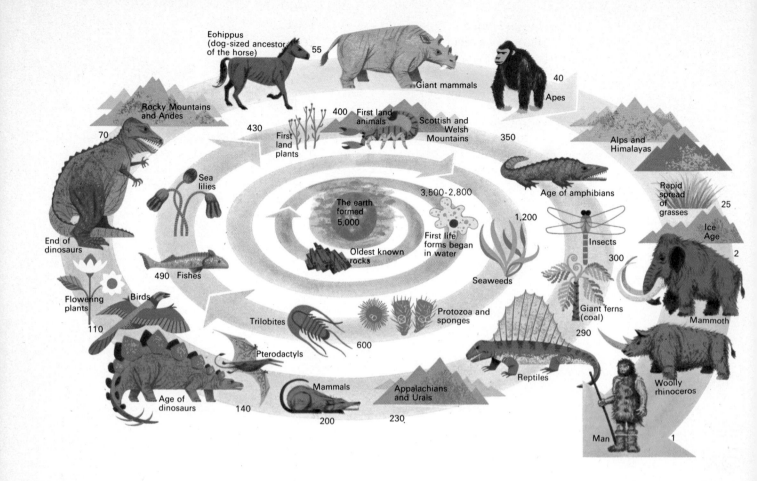

The earth formed 5,000

3,500-2,800 Oldest known rocks

First life forms began in water

600 Protozoa and sponges

Seaweeds

1,200

Trilobites

Fishes 490

Sea lilies

First land plants 430

400 First land animals

Scottish and Welsh Mountains

Rocky Mountains and Andes 70

Eohippus (dog-sized ancestor of the horse) 55

Giant mammals

Apes 40

350

Alps and Himalayas

Age of amphibians

Rapid spread of grasses 25

Insects

Ice Age 2

Giant ferns (coal) 290

300

Mammoth

Reptiles

Woolly rhinoceros

Man 1

Appalachians and Urals 230

200 Mammals

140 Age of dinosaurs

Pterodactyls

End of dinosaurs

Flowering plants 110

Birds

The Age of the Rocks

It was once worked out from events in the Bible that the world began in the year 4004 BC. Several different ages for the world have been suggested. These suggestions have been based on calculations of the time it has taken for life to develop, the amount of salt in the oceans, and the amount of radioactivity in the rocks. Now that the jigsaw has gradually been pieced together we think the earth is between 4,000 and 5,000 million years old.

The rocks have been searched and studied for clues that will help to piece together the history of the earth. Plants and animals that lived millions of years ago remain as *fossils* in the rocks. They tell us what conditions were like at the time when they lived. We can discover how the rocks were formed and what the world was like in those places.

Five thousand million years of the earth's history. The spiral traces the history of the earth since its creation. Important geological events and the animals that lived at various times are marked along the spiral. *The numbers indicate millions of years.*

The geological time scale
The geological time scale shows how the earth has evolved.
1. Look at the time scale.
(a) How many years ago did the earliest forms of life which have been discovered live?
(b) How old are the rocks where the first sponges were formed?

The early rocks are so old and distorted that not very much can be discovered from them. Only a little is known until 600 or 700 million years ago. It is difficult to realise how long ago this was. A diagram will help.
2. Imagine that one year represents the age of the earth. Draw a square for each month of the year. Shade in the squares from January to October. These are the months we know little about. Label them 'Pre-Cambrian time'. Geologists can trace only November and December with any accuracy. Label this period 'The last 700 million years'. It is almost midnight on New Year's Eve before man's appearance on the earth can be drawn on the diagram.

The geological map

From man's knowledge of the rocks, scientists have been able to make geological maps. The map of the geology of Britain on this page has been simplified. It gives a general idea where the different types of rock are found and which are the oldest.

The key to the map is a kind of time scale similar to the pictorial diagram opposite. This is called a *geological column*. Look at this column carefully. The oldest rocks can be seen at the bottom. These are the Pre-Cambrian rocks. The youngest rocks are at the top of the column. Each division is called a *period*.

3. Name an area in Britain where there are Pre-Cambrian rocks.

4. What is the name of the period when the youngest rocks were formed?

5. What kinds of rocks does the key say are found in the Carboniferous period?

6. The map shows the history of the rocks since Pre-Cambrian times. About how many years does that represent?

THE GEOLOGY OF THE BRITISH ISLES

SEDIMENTARY ROCKS

The numbers in brackets show the age of the rocks in millions of years

CAENOZOIC

TERTIARY (up to 70)
Mainly sands and clays

MESOZOIC

CRETACEOUS (70–135)
Mainly chalk, sandstones and clays

JURASSIC (135–180)
Mainly limestones and clays

TRIASSIC (180–225)
Sandstones, marls and conglomerates

PALAEOZOIC

PERMIAN (225–270)
Mainly magnesian limestones, sandstones and marls

CARBONIFEROUS (270–350)
Shales, coal seams and sandstones

Limestones, shales and grits

DEVONIAN (350–400)
Sandstones, shales and conglomerates, and limestones

SILURIAN (400–440)
Shales, sandstones and mudstones, and some limestones

ORDOVICIAN (440–500)
Mainly shales and mudstones, and some limestones

CAMBRIAN (500–600)
Mainly shales, sandstones and mudstones

LATE PRE-CAMBRIAN (600–1100)
Mainly sandstones, conglomerates and grits

METAMORPHIC ROCKS

LOWER PALAEOZOIC AND PROTEROZOIC
Mainly schists and gneisses

EARLY PRE-CAMBRIAN (1600–2600?)
Mainly gneisses

IGNEOUS ROCKS

Intrusive rocks, including granite

Volcanic rocks, including basalt

kilometres

0   100   200   300

Types of Rocks

Rocks can be divided into three main types, or *classes*. These are:
1. Igneous Rocks.
2. Sedimentary Rocks.
3. Metamorphic Rocks.

Igneous rocks

Igneous rocks have a fiery origin. You can imagine the terror of people seeing masses of red-hot, liquid rocks flowing from volcanoes and cracks in the earth. It is not surprising that they called them *volcanic rocks,* after Vulcan, the ancient Roman god of fire. Rocks which pour out on to the surface of the earth in this way are said to be *extrusive.* When the liquid rock cools down, it forms a solid rock called *basalt.*

1. Draw the diagram below, which shows igneous rocks. Write clearly the label 'Volcanic rock, or basalt' in the correct place.

Not all igneous rocks are formed in this way. Some are great masses of molten rocks which have forced their way between other rocks, deep down. These are called *intrusive* rocks. The *batholith* in the diagram is a great mass which was formed in this way. It cooled down slowly and the rock became granite. Sometimes these rocks formed deep down are called *plutonic rocks.* They

are named after Pluto, the ancient Roman god of the underworld.

2. Add the label 'Granite is a plutonic rock' in the correct place on your diagram.

Hypabyssal rocks are another type of igneous rock. These form in much smaller masses, such as the *sills* and *dykes* in the diagram.

3. Write 'Hypabyssal rocks' by the sills and dykes in your drawing.

Liquid igneous rocks are made of various minerals. When the rocks cool these minerals form different crystals. Sometimes the crystals have beautiful shapes. Quartz can be found as crystals like those in the illustration. Quartz takes a long time to wear away, because it is a very hard mineral.

Crystals of quartz

Amethyst

Smoky quartz

Jasper

Citrine

The formation of igneous rocks

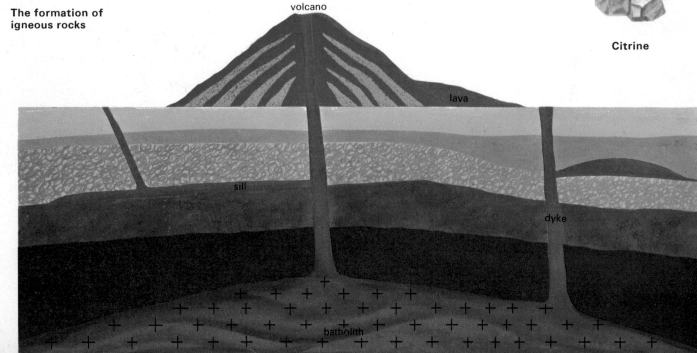

volcano

lava

sill

dyke

batholith

Sedimentary rocks

The rocks are attacked and gradually destroyed by the weather. The loose, broken pieces are carried away and deposited elsewhere by streams and rivers, by the sea, by glaciers, and by the wind. As the deposits become thicker, they form new rock. These deposits are called *sediments*. The new rocks they form are called *sedimentary rocks*.

The bottom diagram on the right shows deposits on the edge of a sea. The pebbles on the beach become cemented together like concrete. This forms a rock called *conglomerate*. The sands are cemented together to form *sandstone*. The fine muds are eventually pressed into *clay*.

4. *Study the diagram on the right carefully.*
(a) How do the sands and muds get into the sea?
(b) Why do you think the mud is furthest from the shore?
(c) What presses the mud into clay?

The map of a delta at the top of the page shows how great amounts of the land are dumped into the sea. But not all sedimentary rocks are formed in this way. Other layers of rock may be made by living matter. Plants have formed layers of coal. The shells and bones of sea life have formed chalk and limestone. These rocks are called *organic* sediments.

5. *Use the illustrations on this page to draw a diagram to show how sedimentary rocks have been formed.*
6. *Chalk, limestone and coal are organic sediments. What are* inorganic *sediments?*
7. *Write out and complete the following statements:*
Pebbles are cemented together to become the rock ....
Sand becomes the rock.............................
Mud becomes the rock.............................
Other types of sedimentary rocks are............

Conglomerate (above) and sandstone (below) are sedimentary rocks.

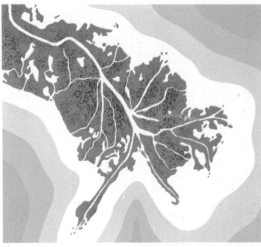

A delta of silt deposited by a river

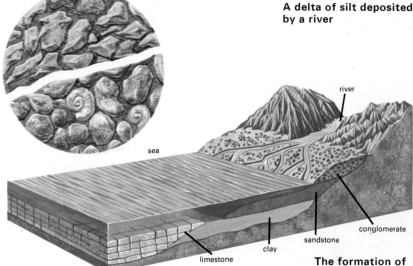

The formation of sedimentary rocks

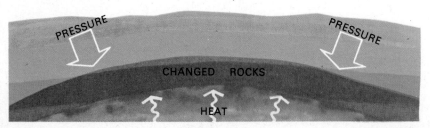

The formation of metamorphic rocks

Gneiss is a metamorphic rock.

Metamorphic rocks

Terrific heat and pressure can change the rocks. Not only the soft, sedimentary rocks but also the hard, igneous rocks can be completely altered. Great pressure builds up in the rocks as they are buckled and folded into mountain ranges. If molten rocks rise up, the surrounding rocks become very hot. In such conditions limestone, for example, can be changed into marble. Clay is pressed into slate, and soft coal into hard anthracite. These changed rocks are called *metamorphic rocks*.

The picture of a piece of rock called *gneiss* shows how even granite has melted and the crystals re-arranged into bands.

8. *(a) Give three examples of rocks which have changed.*
(b) What makes them change?
9. *We can classify rocks into three main types. What are they?*

Dartmoor's Granite Landscape

Granite was formed deep beneath the surface of the earth. It therefore cooled slowly, and the crystals had a lot of time in which to grow large. You can see the crystals in granite with the naked eye. Very hard, clear quartz and shining flakes of *mica* are two of the most important minerals found in granite. Another important mineral which can be seen clearly in granite is *felspar*. Felspar may be white or pink and it gives the granite its colour.

The map of south-west England shows the areas of hard granite.

1. Sketch the map. Find Dartmoor, Bodmin Moor, St Austell and Land's End in your atlas. Name them on your sketch map.

Granite resists the weather because it is so hard. Sometimes it is used as a building stone, but it is very difficult to shape into blocks. In Scotland, the pink granite of Aberdeen is a famous building stone. Look at the photograph above. In Cornwall, the local granite is used to build the harbours of the fishing villages.

In some areas there has been a chemical change in the granite. The change has made it rot and turn into a soft rock called *kaolin*, or china clay. At St Austell, the kaolin is mined and sent to the Potteries area of Staffordshire to make china. The hard minerals which do not rot are washed out. Huge, white heaps of the waste material can be seen on the edge of the moors.

The granite harbour of Boscastle, Cornwall

The granite areas of south-west England

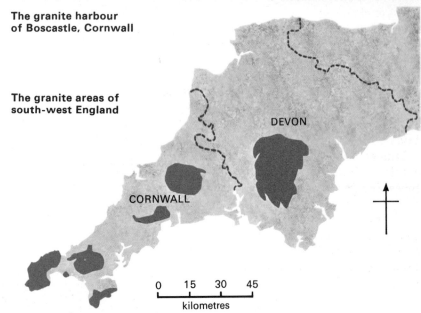

DEVON

CORNWALL

0   15   30   45
kilometres

A china-clay pit at St Austell, Cornwall

Granite is an igneous rock.

2. Kaolin pits can be seen on the left. What are the pyramid-shaped heaps?

3. The kaolin is sent to the Potteries. Where are 'the Potteries'? See page 22.

4. Why do you think granite is used to build harbour quays in Devon and Cornwall?

The granite masses of Devon and Cornwall form large areas of moorland. These moorlands are bleak and boggy and can be dangerous. Rising above the badly drained bogs and marshes are granite hills. Frost, rain, wind and snow attack these hills. But the granite is very resistant, and it defies the weather for a long time. Huge blocks of granite stand on top of the hills. They are called *tors*. A tor rising above boggy ground is shown in the picture on the right.

The Dartmoor National Park lies within this wild and beautiful country. The photograph at the bottom of this page shows some of the moorland, farmland and recently planted forests of Dartmoor. This area is shown on the Ordnance Survey map on the right.

5. (a) How high is Bellever Tor (grid square 6476)?

(b) Give the name of another tor.

6. Use the picture below to make a drawing of a tor. Label it 'A tor of granite blocks'.

7. Give the grid reference of a bog or marshland area.

The rocks of Dartmoor have been used by man since the Stone Age. The ancient *clapper bridges* of the area were made from large blocks of granite. Cattle were kept in stone enclosures.

8. (a) The photograph shows the pre-historic enclosure and hut circle marked on the map in grid square 6577. In which direction was the camera pointing?

(b) How many examples of ancient, stone-built hut circles can you find on the map?

(c) Give the grid reference of an ancient stone bridge.

Minerals such as gold and tin were obtained from Dartmoor in pre-historic times. Many disused mines can be found today. Forests have been planted recently in some parts of Dartmoor. They are a valuable source of timber.

9. Use the map and the photograph to list the ways in which the land is used today.

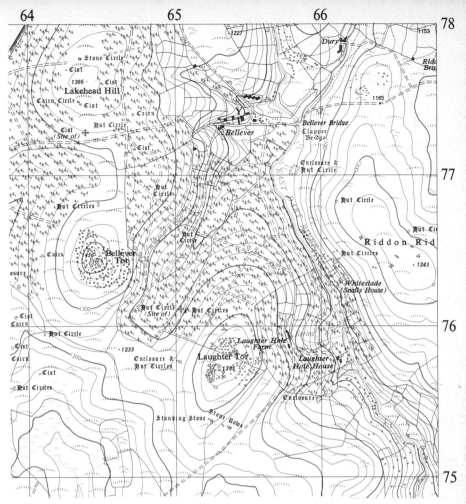

The Bellever Tor area of Dartmoor

Scale: 1:25,000

Crown Copyright reserved

An ancient enclosure and hut circle near Bellever, Dartmoor

The granite blocks of a tor

Sills and Dykes

Whin Sill is a striking feature in the North of England. A *sill* is a roughly horizontal band of igneous rock which has been forced between layers of other rocks. Like the granite of Dartmoor, these sills were formed deep below the surface of the ground. The rocks above were later stripped away to leave the hard sill standing up above the ground. The famous wall built by the Emperor Hadrian to mark the boundary of the Roman Empire stands on top of Whin Sill.

1. Look carefully at the photograph. Why was the wall built there?
2. Which side of Whin Sill is the steeper?
3. Draw a cross section of Whin Sill. Look at page 4. Explain the meaning of the following statements:
(a) Whin Sill is made of igneous rock.
(b) Whin Sill was intruded.

A *dyke* is a vertical band of igneous rock. It is formed when molten rock is forced upwards through a crack. A dyke stands out because it is hard and does not wear away as easily as the surrounding rocks.

4. Draw a plan of the dyke in the photograph. Say roughly how wide it is. The hammer will give you an idea of the scale.

Large numbers of dykes are also found in western Scotland. A large number of dykes is called a *swarm*.

Hadrian's wall marked the boundary of the Roman Empire. It crosses northern England from the east to the west coast. It stands on Whin Sill.

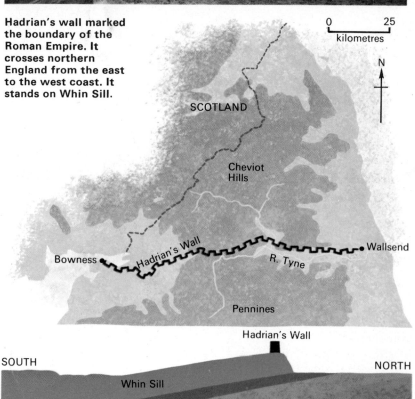

0   25
kilometres

N

SCOTLAND

Cheviot Hills

Bowness — Hadrian's Wall — R. Tyne — Wallsend

Pennines

Hadrian's Wall

SOUTH   NORTH

Whin Sill

A cross section of Whin Sill

5. Look at the geological map on page 3. What do you notice about the types of rocks in the Western Isles of Scotland?

Sills and dykes are quite small compared with large masses of igneous rocks called *batholiths*.

6. (a) What is the name of the batholith found in Devon?
(b) The heat from intruded rocks changes the rocks with which they come in contact. What do we call the type of rocks which have been changed by heat or pressure?

A dyke in Cornwall

Volcanic Landscape

The molten lava which flows from a volcano cools to form a rock called *basalt*. It is made of minerals similar to those in granite. Because the lava cools quickly, the crystals are very small and cannot be seen without a magnifying glass.

The lava from some volcanoes flows out a long way, building a gentle slope. The lava from others does not flow far. Some volcanoes are very violent, some shoot out hot gases, and some build cones of cinders and ash around the vent.

Volcanoes are found where the crust of the earth is weak. They usually occur where there are new ranges of mountains and frequent earthquakes.

1. Draw a diagram of a volcano.
2. From other books, find information about–
(a) the different types of volcanoes;
(b) where volcanoes are found around the world.
3. Use your atlas to find the countries with the landscapes shown on this page.

The volcano shown from the air is in Nigeria. The cone rises from a plateau. The darker patches are lava flows. Fields and villages can be seen further away from the volcano.

4. Draw a map of the area shown in the aerial photograph. Copy the following key beside the map:
A = The crater
B = Cinder and ash cone
C = Lava flow
D = Areas where dust and ash have fallen
Place the letters in the correct places on your map.

The dust and ash thrown out from a volcano often make fertile soils. The lava flows are attacked by the weather and are gradually broken up. Mount Etna is a volcano in Sicily. Villages, farms and villas are built on the old lava flows. In 1971 fresh lava destroyed many homes and much farmland.

5. Study the photograph of Mount Etna.
(a) What use is made of the fertile land?
(b) What do you notice about the edge of the lava?
(c) What has caused the gullies to form?
(d) Is any vegetation growing on the lava?

Mount Etna, Sicily, from the terrace of a villa

Many people live near volcanoes, even though it may be dangerous. Sometimes volcanoes which are thought to be 'dead' are only 'sleeping'. The destruction of Pompeii by Mount Vesuvius in AD 79 is a well-known example of what can happen. When a volcano has stopped erupting, people will move back to the area again.

6. What is the attraction of living in a volcanic area?

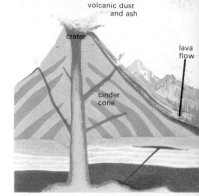

volcanic dust and ash
crater
lava flow
cinder cone

Lava from a volcano in Nigeria, from above

An erupting volcano

The Rocks Exposed

Bryce Canyon, in Utah, U.S.A., is a spectacular sight. The Indians called it Unka-timpe-wa-wince-pockitch — that is, 'Red rocks standing like men in a bowl-shaped canyon'. Ebenezer Bryce was the first white farmer to arrive there. He thought it was 'a dandy place to lose a cow'. The canyon has also been called the wildest and most wonderful scene that the eye of man ever beheld.

1. Of what do the strange towers and pillars remind you?

Bryce Canyon is made of sedimentary rocks which are being *eroded,* or worn, away. Rock towers and small, table-like plateaux called *mesas* rise from the floors of canyons cut into the rocks by the rivers. Fantastic shapes have been created by rain, snow, frost and wind. One of these rock shapes is supposed to look like Queen Victoria. The diagram shows how such rocks were formed. The softer rocks were quickly worn away, but the harder blocks were eroded more slowly and remained perched on top.

Queen Victoria Rock, Bryce Canyon, Utah

How Queen Victoria Rock was formed

Bryce Canyon, Utah

2. Draw the Queen Victoria rock. Shade and label the layers of harder rocks. Label these areas 'sandstone'. Label the softer bands 'clays and shales'.

3. How are rocks eroded away?

4. What eventually happens to rock pillars such as the Queen Victoria rock?

5. Find out the meaning of the following:
(a) mesa   (b) canyon
(c) sandstone (d) shale

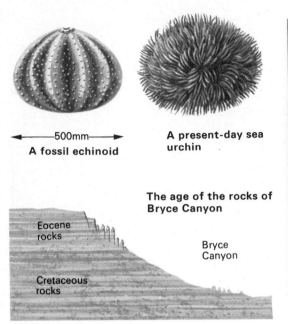

←—500mm—→
A fossil echinoid

A present-day sea urchin

The age of the rocks of Bryce Canyon

Eocene rocks

Bryce Canyon

Cretaceous rocks

The section drawn across Bryce Canyon above shows the age of the rocks. Rocks of this period are also found in Britain.

Geologists can discover the age of rocks by examining the fossils found in them. They do this by tracing the way life has changed as time has gone by. They can also find out the amount of radioactive carbon remaining from their bodies. Living things contain radioactive carbon which decays at

The Grand Canyon, Arizona

a slow but steady rate after they die. Even today some of the radioactive carbon is left after millions of years. The geological time scale on page 2 shows some of the many different types of plants and animals that lived long ago. Their remains have helped geologists to discover the age of the rocks in which they were found.

6. In which parts of Britain are there rocks of the same age as those in Bryce Canyon? Look at the section of Bryce Canyon and the map on page 3.

7. What is the name of the fossil (shown in the diagram) found at Bryce Canyon?

The fossil found at Bryce Canyon was one of the many sea creatures that lived at the time when the rocks were forming. The sea urchin is its present-day relative.

The Grand Canyon is huge. It is more than 300 kilometres long. In some places, it is more than 25 kilometres wide. The river has cut down nearly 1½ kilometres.

8. Study the map and answer the following:
(a) How far is the Grand Canyon from Bryce Canyon?
(b) In which state is the Grand Canyon?
(c) Which river has cut this canyon?

As in Bryce Canyon, the rocks of the Grand Canyon have been worn into strange shapes. The river has cut down through the sedimentary rocks. At the bottom of the gorge are some of the oldest rocks in the world. Scientists can trace 1,000 million years of the earth's history in the Grand Canyon.

The location of Bryce Canyon and the Grand Canyon

UTAH

Wasatch Plateau

Colorado River

Bryce Canyon

Grand Canyon

0   100   200
kilometres

Chalk Landscape

Chalk is a soft, white limestone. It is made of calcium carbonate. This calcium carbonate came from the skeletons of millions of sea creatures which lived in shallow seas 75 million years ago. It formed in clear water where no rivers brought in silt to contaminate it. Chalk is therefore pure.

The white cliffs at Dover and many other parts of south-east England are good places to examine the chalk. Narrow bands of hard flint can be found embedded in it. These bands are where the mineral silica has collected. The silica came from millions of sponges found in the ancient seas.

The chalk rock has produced a particular type of scenery. As the map below shows, the chalk covers a large area of England.

1. Trace or copy the map. Use an atlas to find the following chalkland areas and name them on your map: North Downs; South Downs; Chiltern Hills; East Anglian Heights; Salisbury Plain; Yorkshire Wolds.
2. Look at the geological map on page 3.
(a) Find the areas of chalk.
(b) What do you notice about the Cretaceous Period?

The South Downs at Fulking, Sussex

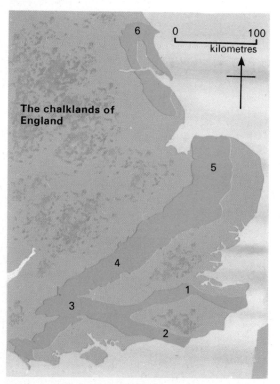

The chalklands of England

0   100
kilometres

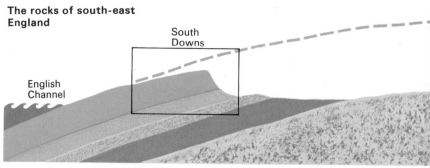

The rocks of south-east England

South Downs

English Channel

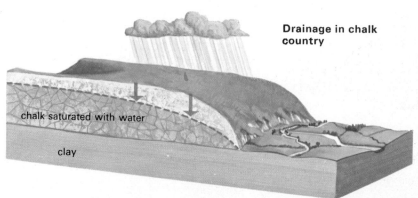

Drainage in chalk country

chalk saturated with water

clay

(c) What sort of life existed at the time when the chalk was formed?

The rocks of south-east England were formed on the bed of a sea. They were then raised up into a dome. The cross section below shows how this dome of sedimentary rocks has been worn away.

3. Make a drawing of the cross section.
4. Which rocks were (a) on top of the dome (b) at the centre of the dome (c) worn away most quickly?

Chalk cliffs near Beachy Head, Sussex

Tyrannosaurus Rex, a fierce animal that lived in Cretaceous times

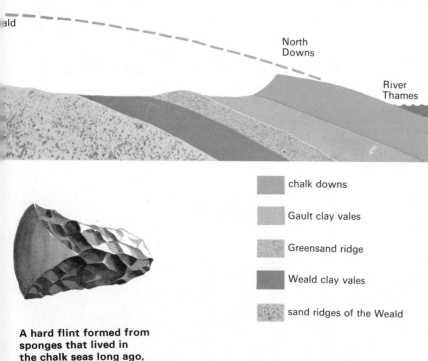

ald

North Downs

River Thames

■ chalk downs

■ Gault clay vales

▨ Greensand ridge

■ Weald clay vales

▨ sand ridges of the Weald

A hard flint formed from sponges that lived in the chalk seas long ago, shaped to form an axe-head

The sandstones and chalk form hills and the clay forms vales. The chalk hills have a distinctive shape. Look carefully at the photograph of the South Downs at the top of the opposite page. A hill of this shape is called an *escarpment*, or *cuesta*. The steep, or *scarp*, slope is marked A. The gentle, or *dip*, slope is marked B. The clay vale at the foot of the scarp slope is marked C.

5. Draw the view in the photograph. Label the clay vale, scarp slope and dip slope.

The chalk hills have a gentle, rounded form and their surface is very dry. Not only the hills, but also many of the valleys are dry. This is because rainwater sinks rapidly into the rock. The diagram at the bottom of page 12 shows how the water passes through the chalk, which soaks it up and holds it like a sponge. The water does not sink through the clay.

The water flows through the rock and eventually comes to the surface again. It emerges as a spring. The existence of springs was one of the reasons for the growth of farms, villages, and towns at these places. A line of villages has grown up, for example, along the springs at the scarp foot of the South Downs.

6. (a) On your drawing of the photograph, mark the village as a 'Scarp-foot village'.
(b) Apart from the South Downs, where else would you find scarp-foot villages in south-east England?
7. The farming and vegetation on the chalk-lands and on the clay vales differ. Copy the chart below. Study the diagrams and the photograph and complete the chart.

Area on Photograph	Description of Vegetation and Farming	Reasons for Differences
A		
B		
C		

Chalk has had several important uses since early times. Stone Age man found the drier chalk hills easier to live on than the clay lowlands. There he found flints which he shaped into arrowheads and axes, his earliest tools. Today, chalk is used in some buildings usually together with hard flint. It is used for lime for the soils of the lowland farms and it is important in making cement.

Limestone Country

During the Carboniferous period limestone formed in shallow seas which teemed with life. Like chalk, limestone is made of calcium carbonate. It is much older than chalk, and is hard and often grey in colour

Water sinks into the limestone and dissolves it. As a result, the surface of limestone country is dry. In some areas the soil is thin and in others bare rock is exposed on the surface. The areas of bare rock, or *limestone pavements,* are made of blocks called *clints.* Between the clints are crevices called *grykes.* Grykes form where the limestone has been dissolved by rainwater.

Streams and rivers that flow onto limestone soon disappear underground. They make their way through underground passages and caves. They reappear at the edge of the limestone area. In time, the underground streams enlarge the caves and passages. Sometimes the roof falls in and a *gorge* is formed. The famous Cheddar Gorge in the Mendip Hills of Somerset may have been partly formed by a series of such cave collapses.

Underground in limestone country there is a maze of connecting passages and caves. Streams do not flow through them all. In many, there are beautiful and strange *stalactites* and *stalagmites*. These are formed

Collapsing caves may have helped to form Cheddar Gorge.

from dissolved calcium carbonate deposited by the water as it seeps through the limestone. These features can be found in various parts of Britain. The map on page 3 shows the most important areas.

1. Look at an atlas and the map on page 3. Where is Carboniferous limestone found in Wales, in Scotland, in central and northern England, and in Somerset?
2. Make a drawing to show the features found in areas of Carboniferous limestone.
3. What is a swallow hole?
4. What is the difference between a stalactite and a stalagmite?
5. Why do you think stalagmites and stalactites cannot form in caves where there are underground streams?

A bare limestone pavement formed of clints and grykes

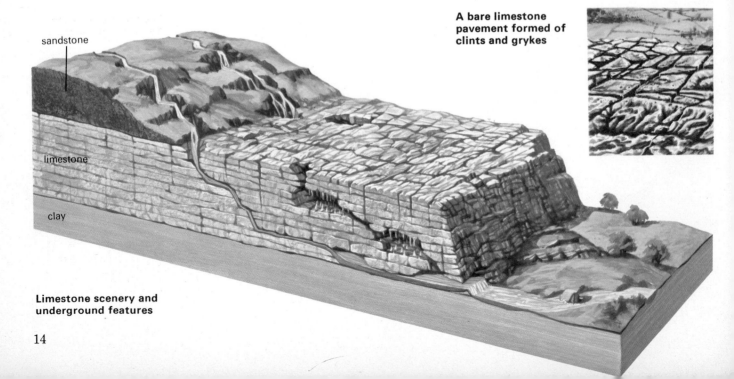

sandstone

limestone

clay

Limestone scenery and underground features

Limestone around the world

Carboniferous limestone is found in many parts of the world. The scenery is often on a much larger scale than it is in Britain. The largest cave in the world is probably the Carlsbad Cavern in New Mexico, U.S.A. About 2 million bats live in the entrance to this cave and fly out every evening in search of food.

Pot-holers exploring caves find many things. They may discover, for example, the remains of extinct animals and of prehistoric people near the entrances and fish without eyes in the dark, underground pools and lakes.

The photograph of Luray Caverns in Virginia, U.S.A., shows the large size of some stalactites and stalagmites. These have joined to form gigantic pillars. The stalactites at Luray are used to play music from an organ in a large cave which is used as a concert hall.

1. How are stalactites and stalagmites formed?

2. In which mountains are the Luray Caverns?

Along the coast of the Mediterranean Sea there are many areas of Carboniferous limestone. There is also a large concert hall in the caves beneath Gibraltar and beautiful lagoons beneath the Isle of Capri. In Yugoslavia, thousands of tourists are carried by railway far into the caves at Postojna.

Postojna is in the Karst area of Yugo-

Inside the Luray Caverns, Virginia

slavia and is marked on the map below. The type of countryside which develops on Carboniferous limestone in other parts of the world is usually called *Karst scenery*.

3. How far is Postojna from Venice in Italy?

4. Look at your atlas and name the mountains in the Karst area of Yugoslavia.

The limestone of the Karst is being worn away. Gradually, it collapses into the caves. The small areas of collapse are called *dolines*. These join together to form a *polje*. A polje is a wide, clay vale.

5. Draw a diagram of the Karst. Label a doline and a polje. Add a note to your diagram to show and to explain which area is best for farming.

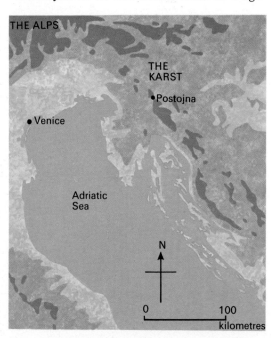

THE ALPS

THE KARST

•Postojna

• Venice

Adriatic Sea

N

0   100
          kilometres

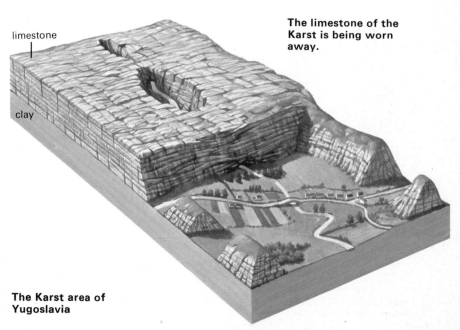

The limestone of the Karst is being worn away.

limestone

clay

The Karst area of Yugoslavia

Pennine Landscape

Many of the features found in areas of Carboniferous limestone can be seen on the Ordnance Survey map of the Pennines. The diagram on page 14 shows these features.

1. Make a drawing from the diagram to show the features found in a limestone area.

2. Find Malham Tarn in grid square 8966 on the Ordnance Survey map. A stream flows from the Tarn southwards. Follow its course.

(a) What happens to the stream at grid reference 895655?

(b) What happens to it at Malham Cove?

(c) Where is the stream between point 895655 and Malham Cove?

The upper photograph, taken above Malham Cove, shows the Pennines and the bare limestone pavement. This pavement is made of clints and grykes.

3. Study the photograph and grid square 8964.

(a) Draw the map symbol used to show limestone pavement.

(b) Draw a sketch to show clints and grykes. What are they?

(c) What causes these features?

(d) What do you notice about the vegetation?

In the Pennines, swallow holes are often called *pots* or *pot-holes*. Not all of them have streams flowing down them today.

4. Find four examples of swallow holes from different parts of the map. List their names. Give the grid reference of each.

Gorges are a striking feature of many limestone areas. The lower photograph shows Gordale Scar in the Pennines.

5. (a) What is the name of a similar gorge in the Mendip Hills?

(b) How were these gorges formed?

6. Find Gordale Scar on the map in grid square 9164.

(a) In which direction was the camera pointing to take the photograph?

(b) Look carefully at the bare rock. Describe its colour and appearance.

Pot-holing is a popular sport in the Pennines. Cavers explore the underground passages and caves. They wear miners' helmets fitted with lamps to light the passages. Ropes are needed to scale underground cliffs and waterfalls.

7. Imagine you have spent a weekend caving in the Pennines or another area of Carboniferous limestone. Describe what you did and saw.

A limestone pavement at Malham, Yorkshire

Gordale Scar, Yorkshire

Calcite crystals

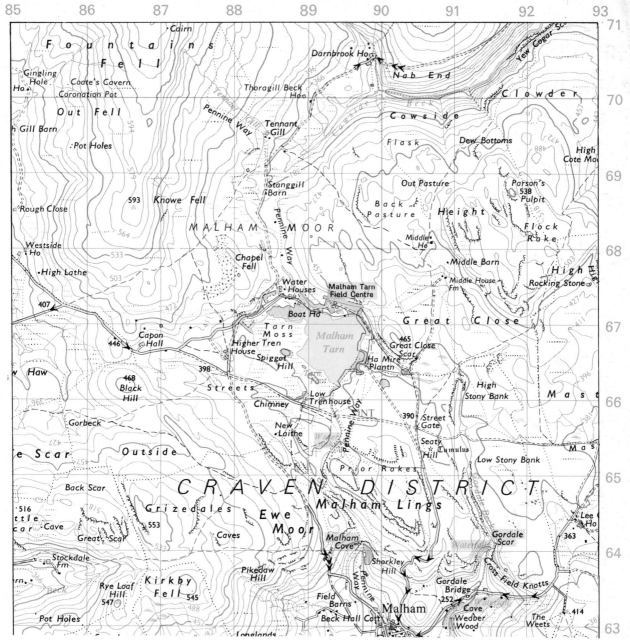

The map might show slight variations in colour from the original published edition

Blue John

The Malham area of Yorkshire
Scale: 1 : 50 000
© Crown Copyright 1976

Blue John is a beautiful mineral. It is made of a type of calcium called *fluorspar*. The piece illustrated comes from the Pennines, where it is found in the limestone.

Lead is found in the *joints* (vertical cracks) in the limestone. It was mined in Roman times on the Mendip Hills. Today, the mines are no longer worked. The limestone itself is used for buildings, and drystone walls divide the fields in the limestone areas. Limestone is also a valuable stone for building roads. As new motorways spread out across Britain, great amounts are being quarried.

A forest 350 million years ago

Coalfields

Fossil remains show what the Carboniferous forests were like.

How coal seams are formed

Fossils found in coal have helped geologists to build up a picture of what the forests were like 300 million years ago. The climate was hot and wet. On river deltas around the sea, there was rich vegetation. There were giant trees of types which are now extinct, club mosses and seed ferns.

Sometimes the sea submerged the deltas and drowned the forests. Layers of vegetation rotted to form peat. Sand and clay were deposited on the remains of the vegetation. Then new deltas formed. This process was repeated time and time again. Layers of vegetation were sandwiched between the sands and clays. Great pressure built up and the peat became coal.

1. The diagram below shows the stages in forming coal. Draw your own diagram to show the layers, or seams, of coal. Add notes to explain how they were formed.

Coal was formed just after the Carboniferous limestone at the end of the Carboniferous period. If you look at the map on page 3, you will see that the coalfields are close to the areas of Carboniferous limestone.

The coalfields of Britain

2. The six main coalfields of Britain are shown on the map above. They are the Scottish, the Midland, the South Wales, the South Lancashire, the Yorks., Notts. and Derby, and the Northumberland and Durham coalfields. Identify them by the numbers.

There are several types of coal. They include soft brown coal, or *lignite,* which does not give off much heat; steam coal; and household coal. A hard type called *anthracite* produces most heat.

In the past coal was the basis of industry. It provided heat and power and many products, such as chemicals and tar. Most great industries grew up on or very near to the coalfields.

3. List as many uses of coal as you can.

Today there are alternatives to coal. Gas and chemicals can be obtained from natural gas and oil. Electricity can be generated in hydro-electric, oil-burning and nuclear power stations. Fewer homes burn coal today than in the past.

4. Why can only the most efficient coal mines survive today?

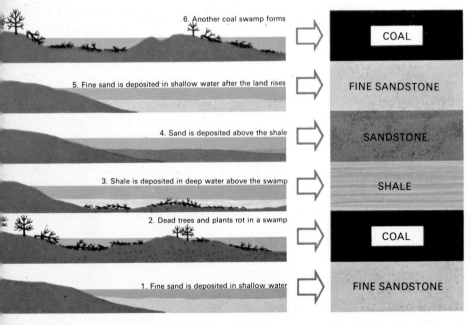

6. Another coal swamp forms — COAL

5. Fine sand is deposited in shallow water after the land rises — FINE SANDSTONE

4. Sand is deposited above the shale — SANDSTONE

3. Shale is deposited in deep water above the swamp — SHALE

2. Dead trees and plants rot in a swamp — COAL

1. Fine sand is deposited in shallow water — FINE SANDSTONE

Coal and iron in South Wales

Coal is mined in the valleys of South Wales. Along the sides of the valleys there are *adit*, or *drift*, mines. These mines were dug where the streams cutting the valleys exposed the seams of coal. The drift mines were the first mines to be worked. Today the coal is obtained from seams deep beneath the valleys. Pit-head gear along the valley floors marks the sites of the shafts leading down to these seams.

5. The valleys of the Ebbw, Rhondda and Rhymney rivers are typical South Wales mining valleys. Find them in your atlas. In which direction do the rivers flow?

Unfortunately, mines and quarries from which our minerals are obtained often ruin the countryside. In South Wales the mining has left great scars in the hillsides. Heaps of waste rock from the mines line the valley sides and tower above the villages. Efforts are now being made to remove them.

6. The photograph shows a typical coal-mining valley in South Wales.

(a) Why were the drift mines worked first?

(b) Why were the houses built in terraces on the valley sides?

(c) What is the purpose of the wheels on the pit-head gear?

(d) For what is the railway used?

7. Draw the diagram of a valley shown on the right. Compare it with the photograph. Label the following on your drawing: drift mines; shaft mines; pit-head gear; pit heap; terraced houses; moorland.

Iron and steelworks used to crowd along the valley floors because iron ore was found locally. Heaps of waste slag still scar the

A colliery in a South Wales mining valley

Obtaining coal in a South Wales mining valley

countryside. The new iron and steelworks are along the coast because the local iron ore ran out. Iron ore and the minerals used for hardening the steel can easily be unloaded from ships. There is also room on the coast to expand.

Iron is made in a *blast furnace*. It is then converted into steel. The diagram of a blast furnace shows the minerals which are necessary to make iron.

8. Copy and complete the following sentences about a blast furnace:

..............is needed as a source of iron.

.... *provides heat.*

.... *is used as a flux.*

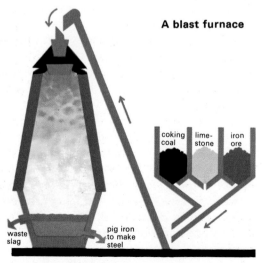

A blast furnace

coking coal   lime-stone   iron ore

waste slag

pig iron to make steel

The Landscape of Jurassic Rocks

Oolite means eggstone. The oolitic limestone which formed during the Jurassic period 180 million years ago looks like fish eggs. It was formed when grains of sand drifting backwards and forwards in the seas became covered in a layer of calcium carbonate. The seas at this time were clear, and corals and sea lilies thrived in them. Sharks and cuttle-fish were plentiful. There were reptiles 8 metres long called *ichthyosaurs* and bat-winged *pterosaurs*.

In Britain, the rocks formed in this period are found from the Purbeck Hills on the Dorset coast to the Cleveland Hills in Yorkshire.

1. Look at the map of the geology on page 3.
(a) How are the Jurassic rocks shown?

The seas in Jurassic times teemed with life.

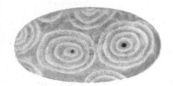

Oolitic limestone looks like fish eggs.

WEST · EAST

The Cotswold Edge near Birdlip, Gloucestershire. In the foreground (below) is a dry-stone wall.

(b) Look at the key. Which other rocks apart from oolitic limestone were formed in the Jurassic Period?

The Cotswold Hills are formed of Jurassic rocks. The photograph at the bottom of this page shows the edge of the Cotswolds near Birdlip in Gloucestershire. The diagram on the left shows the shape of the Cotswolds and the rocks.

2. The Cotswolds have a shape similar to the South Downs. Look at page 13. What type of hill has a steep scarp face and a gentle dip slope?

3. The photograph shows the steep scarp face. In which direction was the camera pointing?

The clay vales are damp and make good cattle pasture. At the foot of the scarp there are springs. Here villages and towns have grown up. The lime washed down from the hills gives fertile loam soils.

The scarp slope is too steep for much farming. There are some limestone quarries and many beech trees. Roads wind up the steep slopes. At the top of the hills, the soil is thin and dry. The grass makes good sheep pasture, but barley is grown in most of the large fields. The broad valleys are often dry. Here the farms are found.

4. (a) Draw a section from the clay vale across the Cotswold Hills.
(b) In which direction does the steep scarp slope face?

5. Read the description of the Cotswold Hills and study the photograph. What would you expect to find at the numbered points on the diagram?

The Jurassic rocks are the most important source of iron ore in Britain. They also provide valuable building stone, for example iron ore is mined in Northamptonshire. The photograph below shows a giant excavator at work. This type of mining is known as *open-cast*. First, the top soil is taken away. Drag-line excavators running on rails then remove the ore. The top soil is returned and the land becomes farmland once more.

Oolitic limestone makes good building stone. The fine grains allow the rock to be sawn freely into shape. The building stones are therefore called *freestones*. One of the most famous is Bathstone. The villages of the Cotswolds, which are built of Bathstone, blend beautifully with the landscape. Brad-

Bradford-on-Avon

ford-on-Avon, shown in the photograph on the left, is an example.

The walls between the fields in the Cotswolds are made of limestone slabs without mortar between them. This is called *dry-stone walling*.

Jurassic limestone is generally used in the construction of only the most important buildings, because stone is expensive to transport. In large cities the limestone is worn away by the weather. Sulphur dioxide from city smoke mixes with the rain to form a weak sulphuric acid. This also attacks and damages the limestone.

6. How were the dry-stone walls shown in the picture built? What type of rock has been used?

7. Freestone has been used in the ancient bridge and buildings of Bradford-on-Avon. What is freestone? What colour is oolitic limestone?

8. (a) St Paul's Cathedral in London is built of Jurassic limestone. Why does the stone-work need constant attention?

(b) The new office blocks surrounding St Paul's are built of cement and iron and steel. Which rocks are needed to make iron and steel? (See page 19.) Which rocks are needed to make cement? (See page 13.)

9. How is iron ore removed from the ground? What is done to prevent open-cast mining ruining the countryside?

10. What kinds of building materials are used in an area you know? Try to find out the age of the buildings. Draw a sketch map to show where they are.

◀ **An open-cast iron ore mine in Lincolnshire**

St Paul's Cathedral and modern office blocks, London ▶

Digging the Rocks

Open-cast mining

Bingham Copper Mine is one of the largest open-cast mines in the world. The excavators are gradually removing a whole mountain. Bingham is in the state of Utah. Many valuable minerals are found in this part of the U.S.A.

1. (a) *From your atlas find out in which mountains Bingham lies.*
(b) *Why is it necessary to mine the copper from terraces?*
(c) *What are the uses of copper?*
2. *Look at this and the next page and pages 19 and 21. Explain (a) an open-cast mine (b) a drift mine (c) a vertical shaft mine.*

Clay pits

Clay pits are a form of open-cast mining. Clay is used for making bricks and tiles; some types are used for making pottery and china.

Stoke-on-Trent is the centre of the Potteries region of England. The coal-fired kilns used to pour smoke across the city. Today the kilns use gas and electricity and are housed in modern potteries.

3. (a) *In which part of England is Stoke-on-Trent?*
(b) *What is made at a pottery?*

Open-cast mining at Bingham Copper Mine, Utah, is on a vast scale.

Fletton brick fields near Peterborough
Scale: 1 : 50 000

© Crown Copyright 1976

China used to be made in old-fashioned pot banks like these in the Potteries

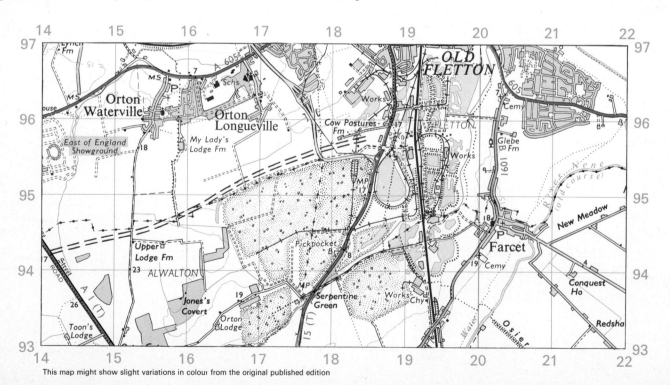

This map might show slight variations in colour from the original published edition

(c) An important mineral is brought to the Potteries from Cornwall and Devon. What is it? See page 6.

Fletton, near Peterborough, is one of the most important brick-making areas in Britain. Huge clay pits and the tall chimneys of the brickworks scar the landscape. One day the brick company must fill in the disused pits and return the area to farmland.

4. How large is the area of open clay pits such as those in grid square 1794? How many pits are now filled with water?

5. How high is the land? What shows this is an important farming region?

6. Why do brickworks need good transport? How are these brickworks well served by transport?

7. Give the grid references for a chimney, a mineral line, a brickworks.

Sand and gravel pits

Sixty tons of sand and gravel are needed to build a house of average size. Much of this sand and gravel was washed out from the great ice sheets during the Ice Age many thousands of years ago. The bones of ancient mammoths and woolly rhinoceros have been found in these sands.

The photograph shows sand pits which have been dug at Chelford in Cheshire. The section shows a patch of sand lying in a clay plain. The table shows how areas of clay differ from areas of sand.

Look at the picture and study the chart to answer the following questions:

8. What use is made of the sand?

9. What happens to the sand after it has been dug out of the pit?

10. Why has the sand pit filled with water?

11. The village in the section has been built on the sands. Why was this better than building it on the clay?

Large sand and gravel pits are found in the sandstones near London. The lakes which form when the pit has been excavated can be quite big. Sometimes they are used as reservoirs or for boating and water skiing. Others are used as rubbish tips.

12. Sand pits are a type of open-cast mining.

(a) Why are they not very deep?

(b) What can be done to stop them from becoming unattractive wastelands?

13. Make a list of the features you would find in the countryside with sandstone rocks. Include those shown in the chart.

A sand pit at Chelford, Cheshire

A cross section of a sand and gravel pit

The Character of Claylands and Sandstone Areas	
Clay Country	**Sandstone Country**
Lowland vales and gently sloping land	Soft sandstone forms gentle hills
Easily flooded	Water sinks in
Water does not sink in	
Many streams	
Cold and damp	Dry and warm
Not very pleasant to live on	Pleasant to live on
Often wooded	Heathland
	Favourite site for golf courses and army training areas
Clay pits for bricks	
	Gravel and sand pits for building (mortar and cement)

Rock Foundations

When it was opened in 1966, the Severn Suspension Bridge was the seventh largest bridge in the world. Its graceful sweep carries the motorway from Bristol across the River Severn to South Wales. The photograph shows the huge anchorage at Aust Cliff and the towers 150 metres high which support the roadway. These towers rest on piers which have been sunk into the rocks beneath.

It was difficult for engineers to find a point where the Severn could be bridged. They finally chose a position where the rocks made good foundations.

The Severn Suspension Bridge

The rocks supporting the foundations

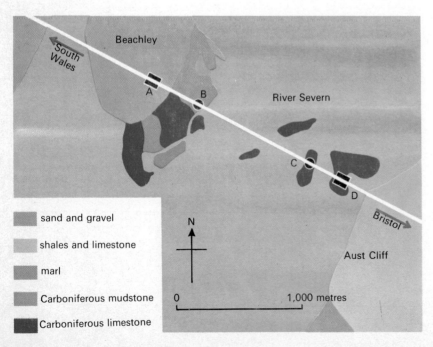

sand and gravel

shales and limestone

marl

Carboniferous mudstone

Carboniferous limestone

0   1,000 metres

1. Look at the photograph and the map.
(a) In which direction was the photograph taken?
(b) The span is over 1,000 metres long. What is the name of the area where it finishes on the north side of the river?
2. Study the map and the cross section. Both show the geology and explain why the site was chosen.
(a) What is the hard rock on which the anchors and one of the piers have been built?
(b) Which anchorage was the easier to build?
(c) Which pier was the more difficult to build?
(d) Why were one anchorage and one pier more difficult to build than the others?

Find the River Severn in an atlas. The estuary is one of the most dangerous in Britain. Rocks, sand banks and strong tidal currents make it difficult to navigate.
3. Where is the nearest bridge to the suspension bridge across the River Severn?
4. What difficulties did the engineers have to consider when they were building the suspension bridge, apart from the rock foundations?
5. Make a list of other structures which need strong rock foundations.

24